A FUNNY THING HAPPENED ON THE WAY TO THE BEACH

True Tall Tales of Zany Animals and Crazy People Making Mayhem in the Mangroves of Florida

Written by

BERNARD RATH

Illustrated by

MARGIT HEISS

DEDICATION

To the tram drivers of Clam Pass and Pelican Bay, past, present and future. Required to serve many masters, they do so with a quip, a smile and aplomb. And to Zero Mostel, and Nathan Lane for showing us the humor in every day comings and goings.

TABLE OF CONTENTS

LIST OF ILLUSTRATIONS

LIST OF ILLUSTRATIONS (CONT'D)

LIST OF ILLUSTRATIONS (CONT'D)

ACKNOWLEDGEMENTS

Thanks to my early readers, especially Art Ritas, Jim Truluck and Sharon Truluck who in the beginning encouraged me to proceed. Later readers Tom Cravens, Neil Billig, Jenny Billig, Jay Giardana, Vanessa Rath Menton, and Lauren Rath made specific and excellent suggestions to help make this a better work. Also to Susan Rath and Ashlee Kelly for lay-out help and especially to Margit Heiss for sharing her splendid talent and making this a much more entertaining book than it would have been otherwise.

CAT TALE

I was driving my stretch golf cart back from the beach to the parking lot late on a spring morning when one of my passengers in a very excited voice shouted,

"Hey, I just saw a panther!"

At an immediate loss for words and searching for an apt rejoinder to the suspected wag in my wide angle rear view mirror I responded to the effect that it was early in the day for rum but it would soon be noon and what the heck he was on vacation anyway.

"No", he protested. "Seriously, I just saw a panther in the woods!"

9

After asking whether he had just returned from the Mile High City of Denver, it became clear from the inflection in his voice that he had indeed seen something notable. I stopped the cart and said "So let's walk back there and check out what you did see". There, barely visible about fifteen yards beyond the boardwalk rail, lying in the muck and detritus among the prop roots of the red mangrove trees was something that could have been an overweight yellow Labrador dog. It looked like Marley of book and movie fame. From that distance it could have been Molson too. Molson was our family dog selected from the litter by my son to become first dog to both me and our young family at the time. He certainly could have been Marley's twin as his sire's name was Trouble. Nowadays our "Granddogs" are a cockapoo named Dunkin; a pair of Great Danes, (one blue and one black named Arthur and Stanlee), and a large affectionate Dane/Black Labrador mix called Clark.

We stared a while longer and my passenger was more adamant than ever that it was a Florida panther. After a minute or two of incredulous staring and wishing I had my other glasses, I reluctantly conceded that I too thought it was a Florida Panther. My reluctance to confirm the sighting also had a practical reason as I was doing mental arithmetic as it related to the ramifications of this highly improbable event which was that of a loose wild panther in the middle of a popular beach during spring break. It was not beyond the realm of possibility that a video I would make of "Cats Gone Wild" could go viral on YouTube surpassing its namesake of "Girls Gone Wild" by millions of views……. or not.

One of the reasons for my skepticism is that there are only 160 or so panthers left in the Florida wild and the authorities generally know where they are as most of them wear radio collars and are monitored regularly from the air. While the 570 acre Clam Pass estuary is pretty wild looking, it s not wild per se as it is located within a larger 2,100 acre neighborhood called Pelican Bay that houses 13,000 mostly seasonal residents, likely all of whom were currently in residence along with their children and grand-children this particular week. One weary resident once commented how she barely had time to launder the sheets and towels as three of her children arrived from the cold northern states in three successive weeks, each of whom brought along a spouse and a gaggle of grandkids. This is a fairly common occurrence in Naples Florida, a wonderful little winter resort town that is as far south as you can drive on the western side of the state before the road turns eastward. If you blink and miss Naples, after 90 minutes of driving, the road will deposit you smack in the middle of Little Havana on the eastern outskirts of Miami. The Pelican Bay neighborhood is located just north of Naples city proper and large enough to operate its own local government services division. In addition to housing the local symphony orchestra and the public art gallery it also lays claim to the only bookstore left in town, as well as the Saks 5th Ave and Nordstrom department stores all less than a half a mile from the mangrove estuary. The area through which we drive is surrounded by ocean to the west with high rises to the south of it, high rises to the north of it and a grid of heavily trafficked four and six lane roads to the east of it.

Male adult panthers have a huge range measured at more than two hundred square miles and as a result of this their biggest cause of death is being killed on the road. On average about two dozen are killed each year on Florida's roads as they try and get to where instinct tells them they would rather be, or where the older alpha-males tell them they ought to go. In addition, during the 1990's the remaining Florida population faced such serious genetic health issues that the authorities engaged

13

in a controversial decision to promote cross breeding with female Texas cougars that were imported as "mail-order consorts." Contrary to popular belief the Florida panther is not black in color. It is a tawny yellow like all the other North American cougars, pumas, mountain lions or catamounts, though it may have black highlights outlining some of its facial features.

My immediate thought was that this panther was in distress and that I ought to call for help. It was well outside of its normal habitat, was not moving except for raising its head periodically and the mangrove muck in which it was lying couldn't have been the most comfortable place to be. Even if it was fine and in good health, the odds of it getting back unharmed to the open range east of town were minimal. It would have had to cross a busy highway, an Interstate and a half dozen deadly six lane regional roads, not to mention countless neighborhoods full of armed Floridians determined to stand their ground. So I made the call.

A few years before I'd met an officer from the Florida Fish and Wildlife Conservation Commission. He was based at Shell Island in the Rookery Bay National Estuarine Reserve way south of town on the road to Marco Island. For whatever reason he had come to Clam Pass Park one day, drove with me to the beach a couple of times, put me on his email list for Red Tide Reports and fishing regulations and told me to call him if I ever saw anything unusual. As it turned out I still had his business card in my wallet. The first call was to the office number and while I was listening to the automated list of options it occurred to me that the panther might take off before I could get through them all, so I hung up and called his cell phone directly. He picked up within a few rings and said he would pass on the information to someone closer to our area. At this point the long arm of government reared its ugly head and I got a call from Miami which went something like this…..

"Hello, did you just call in a panther sighting?"

"Yes, thanks for calling back. I think the panther is in distress. Is someone coming?"

"Are you sure it's not a bobcat? We get a lot of people that mistake a bobcat for a panther."

"No I have seen a bobcat before. This is not a bobcat. I am pretty sure it is a panther. I think it is in distress as it is just lying in the mangrove muck."

"What kind of muck?"

"Mangrove muck!"

"What kind of muck? Spell that please."

"M-a-n-g-r-o-v-e -M-u-c-k"

"What difference does it make, what kind of muck, anyway?"

At this point anyone who knew me in my other life as a high strung, Type "A" testosterone laced alpha-male New York business executive and advocate for the underdog is surely wondering what happened to the old Bernie. The old Bernie would not have let an opportunity like this slip by. A four letter word that ends in –U-C-K just presents way too many opportunities for expressions of exasperation with representatives of our government and products of our sporadically dysfunctional education system. Retrospectively it seems this is proof that Naples has this calming effect on people and after ten years of walking many miles on the beach, gunkholing hundreds of islands and coves and all the while driving more than 100,000 miles in an electric golf cart through the salt scented (some would say smelly) woods, I may finally have found inner peace. That my friends without having had to join a formal religion learn to chant or spend prodigious amounts of money on yoga lessons or Lulu Lemon gear. Consequently I did not verbalize my thought that an employee of FWC really ought to know how to spell mangrove. It was not until some days later that it became clear to me that through no fault of her own there were no mangroves left in Miami proper and perhaps she grew up in a section of town where they had all been paved over to put up a parking lot and even if she had a dollar and half, she wouldn't be able to see 'em, (with apologies and thanks to Joni Mitchell).

It was late March and the first officer to arrive was all decked out in his best official finery. He had a pistol in a nice leather holster, lots of shiny brass insignia, crisply creased pants and shiny shoes and one of those really cool hats that the Royal Canadian Mounted Police wear too. In fact it crossed my mind that perhaps he had come straight from the St. Patrick's parade and hadn't been home yet.

"Man you don't look dressed for this kind of work. Are you sure you want to go into that mangrove muck looking like that?" said I.

"I'm just here to confirm that it's really a panther. We get a lot of false sightings. I've got people to go in there if it is."

I gave him a few minutes to reconnoiter, after which he said.

"It's definitely a panther!"

"So now what?"

"I'm gonna call my people. Likely gonna take a while for them all to get here."

Indeed it did take a while. About two hours in fact during which I continued to drive people back and forth to the beach, stopping on the way to and from to point out the panther in the mangroves and trying to make clear to everyone that this was likely a "once in a lifetime moment". Ironically, now I was on the other side of the discussion and found myself having to convince everyone on the tram that the tram drivers weren't trying to make fools of them and that there was indeed a big cat in the woods. There were four other trams on duty that day and all of us went through the drill with our passengers. All except for one, who was always on the lookout for what I like to euphemistically call a shirking opportunity. If such an opportunity presented itself, i.e. to avoid doing whatever it was that he was being paid to do at that particular time, then he would avail himself of it. In this instance he decided that he was a witness to history and would make himself official driver to the FWC for the duration. His patience was ultimately rewarded as he will likely go down in history as the only golf cart driver to have had a panther on his vehicle. It is definitely a tall tale he can always tell around a campfire.

21

We tried to keep the noise down so as not to scare the cat, but the cat seemed oblivious to all of these people standing around and staring at him from just a few yards away. The situation and set up was such that the cat was alone in the mangrove roots and dozens of people at a time were up on the boardwalk staring at him, as if he were an exhibit. It was surreal in a way, as if we were looking at one of those 19th century dioramas in the Museum of Natural History and he was the stuffed object of our interest. But he wasn't stuffed. He was alive and real and this was the 21st century in an upscale Florida neighborhood. This went on for a couple of hours and over that period of time at varying intervals the FWC Swat team was assembled. The tranquilizer dart shooter guy had quite an extensive kit and a pretty impressive array of medieval looking darts and arrows that would have seemed right at home on the set of Game of Thrones. There was a biologist dude and a couple of runner guys (who likely also had more impressive credentials than I am giving them credit for here) like those government CIA people who went to Yale and could kill you with a strategically placed poke of the thumb and you'd never know it from just looking at them. When they were ready, a couple of them including the dart gun shooter climbed down into the mud on the other side of the boardwalk from the panther. As bystanders, we assumed that they were going to duck under the boardwalk and sneak a little closer to get a better shot. Other members of the team spread out along the boardwalk to direct the panther away from the parking lot and tram station where many beachgoers were gathered, oblivious as to what was going on just a few yards away. I missed some of this action, during my travels but it appears that after two hours of lying in the shade and resting up from the long swim he'd likely made to get to this spot, our panther had decided that given the entire hockey team coming at him from three sides, this outcome was not going to end well for him and he had better get up and leave at last. He high tailed it out of here and started running straight for the tram station, where all of these spring breakers were waiting for their golf cart ride to the beach. Afterwards, we learned that he was a 2 year old, 110 pound male and as he was not wearing a radio collar, he had likely not felt the sting of a tranquilizer dart before either. But instinctively he knew enough to run anyway. And so a bit of mayhem in the mangroves ensued and luckily our trained shooter was indeed well trained and made a clean shot. In a few minutes the sedative took effect ironically in a recently cleared area in full view of twenty or thirty guests of the Waldorf Astoria Naples on the balcony of the poolside restaurant and bar. He was blind-folded, boxed up into a sizeable wooden crate with plenty of air holes, lifted onto the back of the golf cart (previously commandeered and still standing idly by) and brought

out to the parking lot. There he was transferred to a pick-

up truck and driven 25 miles out of town to the Bird

Rookery Swamp portion of Corkscrew Swamp Wildlife

Sanctuary. He was sporting a brand new black radio

collar in his Naples Daily News photographic debut

published the next day!

PANTHER KEY

Florida panthers are known to swim when they have to.
While we have no way of knowing for certain, the one
you just read about likely swam from Rookery Bay
National Estuarine Reserve land which comprises about
110,000 acres in the general area around Naples and
Marco Island. Assuming he made the swim from the
area around Rookery Bay to Keewaydin Island, (a mere
hop and a few "kitty paddles" away) in the early morning
hours, he could have easily been at that location in the

Clam Pass estuary before dawn. It is very unlikely that he would have ended up there via the county road system. In fact, I am never a hundred percent sure I am going to be able to get to that location using the county road system. Likely, he then loped north on Keewaydin Beach, swam Gordon Pass, continued running to Doctor's Pass, traversed it and in a matter of minutes from there, been right where we found him. Unlike this author, who is forever trying to find the perfect beach, panthers are less interested in finding a beach than they are in finding a place of their own, preferably a little high and a little dry. The younger males in particular need to strike out on their own, since they are not welcome to stay where they were born and raised.

We are very fortunate to have so much conservation land available for everyday use in this area. The Conservancy of Southwest Florida whose volunteers conduct free walking tours of the Clam Pass boardwalk in the winter season has had a great deal to do with that. In addition to the Rookery land, there is also the 35,000 acre, Ten Thousand Island National wildlife refuge, forgetting for the moment the 1.5 million acres of the Everglades National Park lands which I tend not to use very often as there is a separate price of admission. There is a boat ramp, operated by the Collier County Parks Department at Port of the Islands which is the last settlement before Everglades City and the national park. The county purchased it for millions of dollars back in the early 2000's when that particular Florida real estate boom was raging and we are now well into another. From scouting the islands on Google Earth, it seemed apparent to me, that a few of these islands had beaches that though perhaps far from perfect, were at least worth reaching. Perfect being in the eye of the beholder it seemed apparent that I would never know, if I never beheld to begin with. So off we went, Gertie and me.

On a particular holiday week-end, one Saturday in May, I hooked "Gertie the Gheenoe'" to my 4-Runner and took the 22 mile trip to the launch ramp. The $75 annual Collier County boat launch sticker is good here, even if it feels like you are in another county. The advantage of this particular embarkation point is that it puts you significantly further into the Ten Thousand Island National Wildlife Refuge once you get out of the approaches. The disadvantage is that the approach is a seemingly long (3.0 nautical miles) no wake zone to get out of the Faka Union Canal. What should take a couple of minutes takes either a half hour or an hour depending on one's definition of a wake. One does this ridiculous slow speed in deference to the manatees and sea turtles and in order not to get a ticket. I saw no manatees but did see a loggerhead sea turtle floating on the surface on my return leg. It would definitely have been vulnerable to a boat prop injury in a high speed zone. The next closest county operated public ramp is at a relatively remote outpost in the south east corner of Marco Island. Known as Goodland, it is home to the famous Stan's Idle Hour Bar, the birthplace of the Buzzard Lope dance. A local T-shirt has "Goodland, a drinking village with a fishing problem" printed on the front which sums it up nicely. Launching here puts you in the water in the northern reaches of the 10,000 islands but it is still only seven nautical miles to Panther Key though you can run these seven miles at full speed. It is worth noting that the Goodland route is in exposed water to the west and south and the Faka Union Canal route was entirely in sheltered water this day in a modest easterly wind. Depending on the direction and velocity of the wind, this might factor into your decision making. I've also used Goodland to approach Blind Pass and Kice Island from the east, a couple of times but took a drubbing on the way back on both occasions when the wind shifted from the south.

The route from the end of the Faka Union Canal out to Panther Key is well marked with navigation markers though there was frequent shoaling and Gertie had to "eat more dirt" than I was comfortable with even when I thought I was well within the marks. Luckily it is all muck down there and no rock so no permanent damage was done despite the wailing and screaming of her little Nissan in protest at being made to eat more dirt than a little engine should.

Panther Key is the very last island on the right as the marked channel enters the Gulf of Mexico. The beach is on the west side, opposite from the channel. At the northern end of this beach, there was a fast in-bound tide that led one to a seemingly tranquil lagoon and then a mangrove tunnel exit from it that I would have liked to explore further. Without my kayak though, I thought better of it. I considered letting the tide take me for an inbound float, which I have often done elsewhere, usually when I can see both ends of the pass and then thought better of that as well, not sure how I was going to get back out while knee deep in mangrove muck. As I was mulling, a very large sting ray brushed my ankle as it scurried to safety. I have done the dive with the sting rays excursion over in Grand Cayman's North Sound but felt more or less fully protected in mask, fins and a wet-suit. Under the circumstances, i.e. nearly naked with 85% skin exposed, I chose not to swim with the sharks (they are related you know). It must have been the time of the year as there were a number of pairs of horseshoe crabs engaging in behavior that I'll modestly refer to as cavorting. They have been around for 450 million years so one would have to assume that whatever it is that they do, they do it very well and such cavorting results in significant dividends for the species.

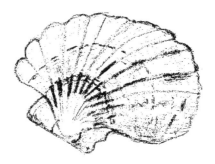

ON GUNKHOLING

Gunkholing is an old sailing term that refers to an activity that takes place once one arrives at an anchorage or landing site. These sites can be coves or islands that may or may not have a beach, but often are muddy, thus the "gunk". That's just another word for muck and interestingly both are four letter words for mud, which with a mere three letters just doesn't suffice for descriptive purposes when you are up to your buttocks in it. In addition, to be true "gunk" and not just mud, there needs to be a definite olfactory component. This is best evidenced by gas bubbles bursting on the surface causing the accidental release of unrecognizable but likely primordial odors that last flew free when dinosaurs roamed the earth.

The "hole" component of the compound word refers to the landing site which is often an indentation in the mangroves that in the classic annals is always a cove, but it doesn't have to be. River mouths and bays, can easily qualify. Indeed one needn't travel far from where I used to drive the beach tram. All three Clam Bays in Naples, (Outer, Inner and Upper) that can be reached from the public parking lot at Clam Pass Park by paddle craft provide lots of gunkholing opportunities. The mouth of the Cocahatchee River, also known as Wiggins Pass is another good and easily accessible gunkholing site locally. All are also terrific for beginning gunkholers as there is a very accessible sandy beach adjacent to the muck where one can get an airing out and even do a rinse and repeat in clean saltwater as often as required.

The verb form of "gunkholing" is a description of an action that I've found is best described (with a slight modification) by Mr. Toad in the classic Kenneth Grahame book, THE WIND IN THE WILLOWS.

"There is nothing- absolutely nothing – half so much worth doing as simply messing about in boats."

My modification is a slight change at the end of the quote so that it might read "……. as simply messing about in the places where boats bring you".

To truly qualify as gunkholing, the "messing about" part ought to have no real purpose. If it does, then of course you are not truly "messing about". Rather, you are tinkering, or fishing or trying to fix something or other, but you are not really gunkholing. A couple of years ago in the Clam Pass Estuary barely a mile as the gull flies from the boardwalk where the golf carts ferry a quarter million people annually to the public beach, I found myself literally up the creek without a paddle. I cite this embarrassing incident to help the reader better understand the various nuances of gunkholing. Even though I was knee deep in gunk, the fact that I was walking a grid pattern while dragging my feet hoping to hook my metal kayak paddle with a foot, eliminates this event as a true Gunkhole adventure. I had dropped the paddle overboard and it hadn't resurfaced. No-one had ever claimed that it floated, but I had mistakenly assumed that it would. Who would make a paddle that doesn't float? After a scary half hour imagining all the different ways I was going to trudge, swim or waddle through the muck to get home without a paddle, all the while avoiding my arrest for trespassing by crack Pelican Bay Security Officers, I kicked it and recovered it. The reason this part of the "messing about in the muck" is not a true Gunkhole adventure is because I had a purpose. I was trying to find my paddle.

The day in its entirety however, was a true gunkhole adventure. On the Clam Pass Canoe and Kayak Trail in Pelican Bay in north Naples Florida, there is a not so secret, secret mangrove tunnel that leads to a cross-over to a magnificent one mile stretch of beach with no buildings on it. Once I entered that tunnel and then landed on a small mudflat through which I dragged the kayak up to hard ground, I was gunkholing.

I walked all of the 35 miles of beaches in the Naples/Marco Island area to get the right feel for my first guide book to the area entitled REACH YOUR PERFECT BEACH IN AND AROUND NAPLES

FLORIDA first published in 2012. I supplemented the walks with kayak and motor boat trips to the islands south of Marco, such as Dickman's, Kice, Morgan, Helen's and others for the second, illustrated edition which came out in the spring of 2015. I am a proponent of gunkholing. Unknowingly I had been doing it for years, always looking for a beach or a small cove or a harbor from Prince Edward Island in Canada's far east to the San Juan Islands in Washington state's far west, that had neither buildings nor people on it. A lot of retirees or semi-retirees golf, sail or play tennis. I have done all of those things and have concluded that gunkholing (until it is discovered and becomes the next big Baby Boomer thing) is the cheapest, biggest, bang for the buck. I can go all day on a gallon or two of gas (or none if I choose to paddle) and find an island upon which I can be "King for a Day". If I choose to rent the island, I inevitably offer nothing in exchange and if there is another person anywhere in sight, I will offer an effective voodoo incantation courtesy of my Haitian co-workers at Clam Pass Park that is surprisingly effective in getting them to leave. One day, I am going to claim an island like those old Spaniards did and see what happens. I will sit on the sand and wait and if someone should come up to me and ask me what I am doing here or where they are, or how to get back, I will just say,

"That will be ten peso's please."

SNAKES ON THE PLANKS

Ordinarily I try not to focus on the snakes in the swamp. Very few people like them and even my hero Indiana Jones is afraid of them. There is a huge "EEW" factor especially among women that is admittedly just not good for business, though generally the kids are fascinated by them. However it is a Florida swamp and Florida swamps are known to have snakes in them so I have always tried to deal with that in a "matter of fact" manner, though I have been known to take advantage of the opportunity from time to time. When looking for snakes most people will look down from the boardwalk into the mud and detritus but they should be looking up.

Most of the dozen or so snakes I have seen have been up in the trees rather than down in the muck. It is when they get down onto the planks of the boardwalk or dangle from the railing that the fun begins. I admit to exhibiting a childish delight when I see them, while pointing them out to people on the tram brings out more of the mischievous boy in me than the naturalist that my passengers seem to think I ought to be because I wear a broad brimmed hat. Inevitably, when asked what kind of snake I saw, (people appear to be rooting for Cotton Mouth and Water Moccasin to score higher on the fear factor of exotic vacations), I feel bound to respond "Do I look like an herpetologist?" That's tough on the passengers as I do look something like you'd expect an herpetologist to look, though I am sure most people have never seen one up close. I certainly feel that when properly posed with the right bones I can be made to look like a paleontologist so it is not a big leap in faith to go from one to the other. If we are not careful this could turn into a bad Henny Youngman routine, who was famous for the "Take my wife…….please" punch-line.

"Geologist, urologist, paleontologist, herpetologist, zoologist, proctologist. I don't know what's the big deal. In the end they're all just gists". Ba ba boom!

When I was a young boy I never had the opportunity to scare the girls at school with a frog in my pocket so perhaps as a recently minted senior this is some long overdue compensatory behavior. If word gets around that I like to prank people like this, I suppose that will interfere with my ability to get into a top shelf senior care facility. It is always possible that the members of the admissions committee will have forgotten why it was they were going to deny me though.

As one drives to the beach, we have what the tram drivers call a "Snake Condo" on the left side of the boardwalk just after the first curve. It is a snag of a dead tree with an amputated limb that has a pair of really neat holes in it, one below the other in which a corn snake or two may periodically take up residence. The bark around the perimeter of the upper hole is worn smooth from the snakes wrapping themselves around the limb. One year there was a snake head in each of the holes for quite some time and rather than hanging their laundry out they'd hung out their recently shed skins. On a particular morning two power walkers stopped for a conversation right at the snake condo with their backs to the holes. While they were talking, the two snakes in residence appeared to become increasingly annoyed and began a cobra dance with their heads undulating outside their respective entrances. At the time I wondered whether it was the content of the conversation that got them annoyed or just the noise itself at such an early hour. After all, the snakes had likely been out all night hitting the boards. All the while the conversationalists were oblivious to the snakes' presence. I enjoyed the show so much I never did tell them to turn around to see who was listening in on their private conversation in the woods.

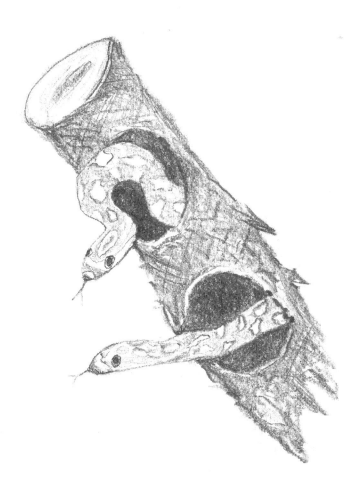

People who ask about the snakes appear to be interested in what kind they are and whether or not they are poisonous. Most of the snakes I have seen are corn snakes, also called rat snakes or red rat snakes because they eat the palm rats not because they look like them. They are native to the country and Florida and are not poisonous. Of course I have no way of knowing whether I have seen a dozen or so different snakes or if I have seen the same snake a dozen or so different times. Did I mention that I was not a herpetologist? This always makes for some interesting word play in response to reptile queries when depending on the time of day or my friskiness the response can take different forms.

"Are there any snakes in here?"

"Are there snakes in here? Are you kidding me? Do bears live in the woods? I've seen dozens of them. This is a Florida swamp you know. What else would you expect?" OR

"Yeah, there's one but he doesn't come out much. I only see him about once a year."

It's the same set of facts but each response generates a totally different reaction. When the corn snakes are coiled around a branch overhead they look relatively benign, at least to me. Though I didn't see this myself, one tram driver reports that the branch around which a corn snake was wrapped, broke and the snake fell to the deck along with it. Two people who were walking together in the same direction nonchalantly parted to the left and right as if on cue and blithely continued on while the snake slithered away. Of course when they are not coiled and on the move the size of the snakes becomes an issue. The Clam Pass boardwalk is just over 3,000 feet long but it is only ten feet wide. One dusky evening as I made the blind left turn over the bridge to the hotel pool I had to screech to a halt as a corn snake the length of which encompassed the entire width of the boardwalk undulated to wherever it is that snakes seem to go at night. They do appear to sleep all day so that they can go out at night. My guess would be that they are out hunting those rats but for all I know they might all go to the Blue Martini equivalent for snakes in Pelican Bay.

"Hey baby. Come here often?"

"Not really but I'm shedding and am itching to get out. Do you like my new color?"

"Love it! Want to writhe?"

Many guests are fascinated by the proliferation of pythons in the everglades which they have seen on the nightly news. They often mistakenly ask about the boa constrictors, when it is the Burmese Pythons that make the headlines. Generally it seemed reassuring when they were told that the closest python to Clam Pass Park was captured about 15 miles away just beside the road to Marco Island also known as Collier Blvd. That was until recently when Jim Truluck, one of our regular Conservancy of SW Florida volunteer guides and a couple of his friends discovered a dead one on Keewaydin Island, so now they have come to within eight miles of this particular park. Pythons are considered an "invasive species' by the authorities in Florida who decide such things. Species are considered merely "exotic" so long as their presence is benign. If the species begins to exhibit behavior or traits that threaten indigenous species then they become "invasive" and can be eradicated. In the case of the Burmese Pythons, the media at one point hyped that there were more than 100,000 of them loose in the everglades and that they were feeding voraciously on the eggs of native species there potentially doing them irreparable harm. FWC sponsored a bounty program to encourage Florida hunters to bring them in dead or alive and only about 60 or 70 of them were reported killed or captured. The source of the pythons is still a mystery. Depending on who is telling the story they are either descended from the reptiles which escaped from the Miami Zoo after Hurricane Andrew in 1992 or they are descendants of those released by disenchanted pet owners who could no longer afford the food and rent to house the cute little monsters they brought home from the pet store a few years before. It's likely a combination of the two.

I'm afraid it is just a matter of time until one morning someone on a tram shouts out "Hey I just saw a python". The driver ought to be far less flippant this time around, than I was with the panther.

I was privileged to witness how an exotic species establishes a foothold in a new country on a new continent a few years ago. Late in 2005, Hurricane Wilma brought 135 mile per hour winds to our neck of the woods and stripped all the leaves from the mangrove trees in the Clam Pass estuary. It was a surreal sight when we returned to work a week later and could see the beach more than half a mile away while driving through the denuded spindly mangrove woods. In addition to a bunch of things, Wilma created the need for a whole lot of new roofing. Most of the red clay roof tiles that adorn so many of the Mediterranean and Tuscan inspired buildings in this region are imported. One morning on the great Crescent Beach of Marco Island as I watched a monster crane raise a pallet of clay tiles to the top of an 18 story building, a big red and yellow snake jumped from the pallet to the beach and slithered into the shelter provided by the sea oats at the dune line. The pallet was clearly marked, "Product of Venezuela". The snake moved too quickly for me to tell if the classic adage "Red to yellow kills a fellow while red to black is a friend of Jack" applied in this case but thinking about this event over the ensuing years leads me to a grim conclusion. This snake, (let's call it the Orinoco Outlaw) apparently came here without a mate. If after a decent interval its period of snake celibacy ends and it finds a Florida native Coral Snake for a mate, then the existing color combination adages are likely to mean little or nothing. It is going to really mess up these little life saving ditties to the point where they will become completely useless like the one about "Feeding a cold or starving a fever" or is it vice versa? "Red to Yellow is mellow. Black to red makes you dead?" The progeny of the Orinoco Outlaw

are likely to be snakes of a different stripe.

My favorite snake story occurred one Valentine's

Day night. As the father of two lovely daughters I have

never once interfered in their choice of dates, but faced

with this event I might have become an activist. When a

boy invites a girl out on a date for Valentine's Day,

where he takes her ought to count for something. If one

of my daughters' dates asked her if she would like to

spend Valentine's Day night walking for more than a

mile in a bug infested swamp at sunset instead of at a fine

restaurant sipping champagne or prosecco, I would

expect her as an intelligent young lady to quickly re-

evaluate this relationship and determine that it might

have limited potential. But here was this nice young lady

escorted by a fine looking young man who declined a

ride in the dusk so as to spend more quality time in the

swamp alone with his date, and it was getting dark

quickly as it always does at Latitude 26 where we reside. Just past the snake condo on my outward bound leg, sat a great big coiled corn snake, obviously relishing the heat of the plastic planks after a cold February day. On my last leg of the day returning to the hotel, who should be right around the next corner, ready to step on the coiled snake but our "Mr. Obviously NOT Right" and his lovely Valentine's date. Now "Mr. Right" had already previously turned down my offer of a ride and I really did not want to mess up whatever progress the guy thought he was making on his "swamp date" but I thought that if the girl stepped on the snake it would definitely be a life changing event. Despite the imp in me and my strong desire to teach this young man a lesson to mind his elders I stopped the tram.

"Excuse me. I hate to interfere with your romantic stroll in the woods, but I have to tell you there is a big snake on the boardwalk right around the next corner."

He, in a kind of a smug sneer, "Sure".

She...."Really? Where?"

Me...."If it's still there, it's just around the next corner. I saw him on my last trip out to the beach when I went to lock up."

She in a very high pitch...."Oh my God. Let me on the cart!!"

And so it was that we passed a foot or two left of the coiled snake languidly absorbing the heat of the day from the warm plastic planks of the boardwalk. I expect the young man had some explaining to do back in the parking lot before he got to first base on that fine Valentine's Day night.

KEEWAYDIN ISLAND

The most exciting thing about this island is that it is so

boring. Hardly anyone lives here and except for a few

holiday week-ends and one big party week-end at the end

of May at the far southern extremity, relatively few

people come to my favorite spots. While there are 50

platted private lots on the 8 mile long island, (six of them

are owned by members of one family) fewer than half of

them have been developed. Those that have been are for

the most part unobtrusive and located well behind the

beach, likely for convenience to the dock for groceries

and supplies and for safety from inclement weather coming off the open sea. Large expanses of the beach are unsuitable for development in any case as lagoons to the east leave little if any room for septic systems or functioning artesian wells. The most southerly of the private homes on 5 acres was recently listed at slightly less than $3.0 million and purchased by a member of the Joe Biden family a few years back. A number of lots were purchased by various conservation agencies and much of the island falls within the Rookery Bay National Estuarine Reserve.

Earlier known as Key Island, the name was changed to Keewaydin Island in reference to the Longfellow poem "Song of Hiawatha". While almost everyone who went to elementary school likely knows the opening lines of this long narrative poem

" By the shores of Gitchee Gumme, by the shining big sea water"

Few pupils likely delved deep enough into the poem to discover these lines.

"I am going, O Nokomis,

On a long and distant journey,

To the portals of the Sunset.

To the regions of the home-wind,

Of the Northwest-Wind, Keewaydin"

This particular wind is considered an ill wind, likely because it makes the water rough and the air cold when it blows. In the case of the Gulf of Mexico for example, the straight fetch of the waves from the Texas/Mexico border to Florida is about 1,000 miles. In the middle of winter, when blowing from the southwest, the wind brings air which has previously passed over Colombia, Curacao, Cancun, Cozumel, the Cayman Islands and Cuba. I like to call that a "C Breeze". When blowing from the northwest it has previously passed over

Colorado, New Mexico, Oklahoma, and Texas. I just call that nasty.

I can personally attest to the ill nature of this wind as one February, accompanied by an original Darryl, (see Chapter 7) we tried to motor a 28 foot sailboat from Boot Key Harbor at Marathon Florida, back to Marco Island, a distance of about 90 miles. We motored into the teeth of just such a wind blowing at 20 to 30 mph. We left at ten in the morning and by nine that evening, it became clear to us that we likely didn't have sufficient fuel to make Marco. We diverted to the Indian Key Light and then travelled down the channel in the pitch black to Everglades City where ultimately we spent the night hard aground on an oyster bar. So that's they called it an "ill wind" even up in Michigan and Ontario where Hiawatha lived. There it comes from Manitoba, Saskatchewan, the Yukon, the Northwest Territories, "for Pete's sake, eh?" Around here, it totally messes up a Florida winter vacation. If you want to test this without putting yourself in danger, just head for the deck at Clam Pass Park when one of these is blowing at 20 knots in February. Bring a parka and a thermos and see what it feels like for yourself. The only difference is you are not getting splashed with 60 degree water every thirty seconds, but you'll just have to imagine that, unless you can get Winston the bartender to squirt you with a hose.

Keewaydin Island was renamed by the operators of a series of "Outward Bound" type sleep-away camps called Keewaydin Camps. These camps, fourteen in all at their zenith were located in Vermont, Maine and Ontario among other places. One of them, founded in 1893 appears still to be operating in northern Ontario at Lake Temagami. As I was researching their website I was surprised to find that it is located just 100 miles by bush plane from where I earned my Boy Scout canoeist merit badge in Algonquin Park. That episode evokes a fond but painful memory in that I had to carry a canoe that seemed to weigh much more than me for a 100 yard portage connecting Smoke Lake to Grape Lake without putting it down. Until the recent availability of Google Earth, I had been under the mistaken impression for more than 50 years that I had carried that canoe for a mile, i.e. 1,760 yards, not a mere hundred. I apologize to all for my past inadvertent "Bunyanization" of that portage. It sure felt like a mile. Not only had I whittled my own paddle from a piece of redwood plank but as a communal project with the rest of the troop we shaped the canoe from fiberglass matte and resin on a group owned

mould. We'd made six of these craft and naturally they

improved as we got better with experience. With the

canoe on my aching shoulders it soon became apparent

that I must have been carrying the first one built and that

we had used way too much fiberglass and ought to have

spent another day or two sanding it away.

When the Keewaydin Camp on Key Island closed as

a result of financial difficulties traced back to the Camp

Director and his spouse's misallocation of funds, the

facility was converted to a lodge. It was listed on the

National Register of Historic Places in 1987, closed in

1999 and is now privately owned.

Despite its apparent seclusion, depending on wind

and tides, this island is readily accessed from various

embarkation points in the Naples area. If you or a friend

has a boat with a motor you can be there in minutes. By

paddle it is generally less than a one hour trip with a

favorable tide to three different landing areas. The southern tip of the island is easily accessed from the free Shell Island boat launch, where Henderson Creek and Rookery Bay meet near Marco Island. This launch area can also be used to access the center of the island near the red navigation marker 46, in the inside channel that connects Naples Bay to the Marco River. There is a shell landing on the channel side and a short twenty yard walk to the beach on the other side. This spot is particularly impressive as when you get to the beach on the west side, you can see nothing but sand, water and vegetation for four miles in either direction which is very much my idea of a perfect beach. Lastly there is a back way through the mangroves to access the north end of the beach, just southwest of Dollar Bay. The closest boat launch is from Bayview Park, but a launch fee is required here. More specific directions can be found on my blog but feel free to scope out the island on Google Earth and get your own

personal feel for the route before setting out.

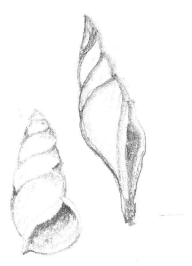

FISHY TALES

If telling people about the snakes that live in the mangroves is not good for business, then telling them about the sharks that live out in the Gulf of Mexico is even worse. For one thing, people are just passing through the woods and will have left the perceived peril behind them in three or four minutes. However they are planning to be at the beach for a few hours and the thought of sharks is likely to linger a lot longer. I don't know why they think there ought not to be any sharks in the Gulf of Mexico. Maybe they think that the Gulf is not a "real" ocean, as I often get questions, such as "What kind of fish do they catch here?" Generally over the years, I have downplayed the threat of sharks at this beach by saying things like "there has never been an incident" or "I've walked at least 50 miles of beaches in this county and never seen one" or something to that effect. One fine morning I pulled in to the tram passenger pick up area at the beach with seven or eight people from somewhere else who were looking forward to a great day at the beach that likely included some frolicking in the water. Lying there on the steps was a four foot long, headless Black Tip Shark. Needless to say the people on my tram had serious second thoughts about going to the beach that day. So it was with the lament of the passing of an era that I reluctantly allowed the local fisherman to place the decapitated carcass of his freshly caught shark on the rusty rear metal platform of my tram. During the trip back to the parking lot we had an interesting conversation during which it was revealed that the head had been sacrificed to the harvesting of the teeth for jewelry and the carcass we were hauling to the car was expected to furnish a large number of steaks for the freezer. According to state regulations, licensed Florida fishermen are allowed to keep up to one Black Tip a day. The regulations include a polite request that all sharks be released on their own recognizance but many local fishermen don't trust sharks to live up to the terms of their parole so they make a point of eliminating

them within the rules. Besides, the appeal of a couple of thousand

dollars worth of fine tasting free protein (though possibly

containing high levels of mercury) can be overwhelming.

The most prevalent fish species in this area are silver and brown

mullet and they can be seen in the water almost every day. As

bottom feeders, they are not predator fish which means they won't

take bait and generally need to be caught by cast net rather than a

hook and line. On one fine evening, while parked at the Rube

Goldberg inspired drawbridge, (that I ineffectually continue to try

and make famous as in Brooklyn and Golden Gate) I was treated to

a spectacular sight of a 50 to 60 yard long run of spawning silver

mullet winding their way northward and occupying the complete

width of the kayak channel. It was a very special sighting and I

have never seen it since. To the south of the bridge, there have been porpoises herding mullet onto the mudflats and at various times though rarely, otters and manatees. The latter have been known to get stuck in the mud and on occasion someone determines that help in the form of helicopters and dozens of volunteers needs to be called to help nature along the way, rather than just wait for the turn in the tide.

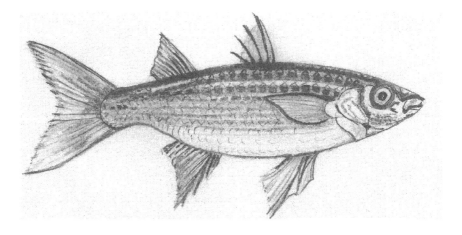

My favorite fish story involves a flying fish. Well, actually it was not flying so much as falling. An apparently athletically inclined young woman recently returned from the beach was unlocking her bicycle from the rack which was just a couple of yards away from where I was sitting in my tram. My vehicle was parked in the roundabout by the gazebo, while waiting for more passengers to drive out to the beach. To the uninitiated it might appear that I was merely lollygagging. When people see me in such a state they inevitably feel the need to volunteer commentary on my choice of "late-life" careers or as I like to call them "senior jobs". When one takes into account that people often mistakenly think that the Tram Drivers are government employees, the situation becomes exacerbated. Generally I say things like, "Well, yes, it beats being a Walmart Greeter", though now that they make higher wages than tram drivers and get an employee discount I might have to reconsider that retort.

"So is this all you do all day? Sit here in the shade on a golf cart?"

"Yes, pretty much. Thanks for asking. It keeps me from becoming a ward of the state by deferring my social security payments one year at a time. I am doing my bit for society by delaying my gratification so future generations can benefit."

"This is a nice retirement job."

"Do I look retired? I'm workin' here! I'm driving an electric bus in a public park and getting kicked and poked in the back by whiny kids or cursed at by under-aged drunkards who want to smoke or make-out on the rumble seat as if I were a horse carriage for hire in Central Park."

"Do you give rides to the beach?"

"No actually, the other drivers do that. As the senior driver on duty today, I'm designated to drive around and around the gazebo and make sure that people are safe from falling objects and standing in the correct place in line."

"I just got hit in the head by a fish!" shouted the athletically inclined lady a few yards to my right.

"What? Are you kidding me?"

"No seriously, I just got hit in the head by a fish from the sky. It fell out of the air and hit me right in the head!"

Abruptly and appropriately my lollygagging came to an end and I resumed my prescribed circle around the gazebo, with one arm outstretched, my head outside the tram looking skyward, laughing and shouting,

"Well where's the manna? We're waiting for the bread!"

Of course, it wasn't until some research a year or more later that I realized (as I'm sure you already knew) that I was mixing up the Old and the New Testament with respect to miraculous biblical fish and bread food stories. Perhaps the idea of food falling from the sky just overtook my imagination though I did think myself terribly witty at the time.

There on the parking lot pavement next to the lady and her bicycle was a foot long, shiny silver mullet. After we had dispensed with the Biblical implications and given the lack of any visible locusts, we concluded that it must have been dropped by an osprey. The other alternative really wouldn't stand up to scrutiny as there was no accompanying bread or manna and it is not like HIM to make that kind of a mistake. I mean HE is a senior but we don't expect HIM to have those "moments" like the rest of us. Some scientists have posited that an osprey's talons will release their prey by reflex if the fish in its grasp is so large that it might affect the raptor's ability to navigate or stay aloft. So nature triggered that response and the agile bicyclist just happened to be standing in the right place at the right time.

As we parted company I suggested that the lady immediately buy a lottery ticket as the odds of winning the lottery were in my opinion significantly better than getting hit in the head by a fish. My theory was that if she was able to beat the astronomical odds of getting hit in the head by a fish, then picking a winning lottery number was going to be a piece of cake. It appears I was mistaken about that too as a subsequent search of the internet revealed that in Florida where flying raptors that like to fish such as Osprey and Bald Eagles abound, their grasp apparently exceeds their reach more often than an unsuspecting reader might expect.

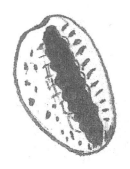

FITZBERNARDO

In February of 1988 six city slickers from New York, Chicago, Toronto, New Orleans and Milwaukee cast off into the wilderness, north and east of Islamorada on a rented houseboat named the "Roger B". The motley crew comprised Bill Rickman, Kevin McCaffrey, Joe Friedman, Chris Keen, David Schwartz and me. We were all booksellers and had finished a series of meetings in Miami for the ABA (American Booksellers Association) and most of us were in no rush to return to winter weather. At the end of the voyage everyone received a souvenir paper chart of the route and the location of the three overnight stops along with a couple of photographs. It wasn't a real chart, but one of those paper placemat maps that one used to get in touristy restaurants and diners.

A Funny Thing Happened On The Way To The Beach

From October 1982 until May 1990 the funniest situation comedy on television was simply called "NEWHART" and the lead character, played by Bob Newhart, was an owner of a small Vermont Inn. My good friend in high school, Les Potapczyk was on to him as early as the mid 1960's, as he owned vinyl albums (LP's) of Newhart doing his comedy sketches even then. Newhart was best known as a stand-up comic whose signature acts were one sided telephone conversations. Prior to his Vermont innkeeper role, he had a long successful run playing a psychiatrist in a previous series a decade earlier. Most regular characters on the new show such as Tom Poston were hilarious deadpans and among them were three brothers. The brothers were somewhat simple to put it mildly and played beautifully to Newhart's style. When the brothers were first introduced to Newhart the innkeeper, the dialogue went like this.

"Hi. I'm Larry. This is my brother Darryl, and this is my other brother Darryl."

If you would like to watch this historic introduction, the clip can be found on You Tube.

After a series of mishaps, misadventures and plain stupid tricks it became clear to the members of the motley crew of the "Roger B" that they had more in common with the Darryls than with Jacques Cousteau and so that is what we called each other for the duration of the voyage and as it turned out for the duration of our lives. To each other, each of us is his brother Darryl even to this day. A handful of other Darryl adventures and misadventures followed this including a pedestrian crossing of the Mexican border at Yuma AZ where nocturnal helicopters searching for soggy-spined swimmers in the Alamo canal reminded us of the movie Apocalypse Now as Schwartz barbecued his signature rack of lamb with garlic and rosemary oblivious to the chaos around him. In addition there was a hike along the ridge of Catalina Island above Avalon and a sail boat charter in the San Juan Islands with a bar run to Friday Harbor.

We loaded up with beer, booze, groceries and cigarettes in Islamorada which is about equidistant between Key Largo and Marathon. A much greater percentage of people smoked in those days (myself included) and Chris who was from Toronto had Export A's which were right up there in intensity and strength with the Gitanes and Gauloises of France. Joe Friedman and I soon thereafter quit smoking with the help of a New York psychologist who used hypnotic therapy. I mention the cigarette pack which was bright forest green because none of us had navigation instruments. Over the next few days the straight edge of the hard pack of Canadian cigarettes became our parallel rule to connect marks on the placemat. These marks were gleaned from the red and green navigation markers that mysteriously and miraculously appeared from time to time out of nowhere. And so was born a new sailor as Kevin wielded the cigarette pack like a surgical instrument and plotted courses that could have taken us to Cuba if we'd had a bigger placemat. These days Kevin is an award winning documentary film maker in New Orleans. He lives 13 1/2 feet below the levee of Lake Pontchartrain and as a result must be the only person in the world to race his J24 sailboat past his own rooftop. Chris drove the boat as he had some experience with power boats on Canadian lakes. I was strictly a sailboat guy and any engine over 8 horsepower was likely to induce vertigo and blood rushing to my brain. I was put in charge of music and played the recently released album by Paul Simon called

"Graceland" over and over again at loud volume and I still associate "The Boy in the Bubble" with green, milky water, wind, waves, dolphins and Darryls.

We didn't know it then, but we were zigging and zagging and burning cheap gas to no end in and around the Intracoastal Waterway (ICW) that connects Miami to Key West on the "Bayside". I have no idea how we ever found where we were going, let alone how we found our way back. In retrospect, since we weren't really going anywhere, it didn't matter much when we got there, which is entirely consistent with gunkholing in general and the brothers Darryl in particular.

Sometimes it just takes a couple of decades to put things into perspective. Twenty six years later, while planning for a Florida Keys adventure with my boat flotilla consisting of Gertie and Jazz, I came across the name of a body of water I recognized from somewhere. When doing preliminary research into a new adventure I often rely on Google Earth. By mapping out a route using the "Tools" feature, I get an idea of distance primarily for time and fuel consumption calculations and whether a day trip is even feasible. Additionally, the retained visual image allows me to form a mental impression of the area. Later if weather conditions change, or I lose my chart or GPS (all of which have happened), the research is reassuring, in the sense that even when most of the islands look alike, that Key at that location should be XYZ Key. For this particular adventure I chose to use the bayside waterfront Hampton Inn at Key Largo as my base, since as a Tram Driver at Clam Pass I was technically a Hilton hotel employee and could stay at any Hampton Inn for $29.95 a night. You can't even pitch a tent in Bahia Honda State Park in the Lower Keys for that amount. Just like frequent flier miles though, available dates are hard to find, so in this case I just kept searching and searching on-line well into the future for a 2 night window. Suddenly, voila, a two night opening appeared and I grabbed it. There was a slight work-around required as the hotel did not have its own boat ramp and I would have to launch at the nearby Caribbean Club. The location is famous for its connection to the John Huston movie "Key Largo" which starred Humphrey Bogart, Edward G. Robinson and Lauren Bacall. Because of the movie connection, it's a sort of touristy biker bar, if there is such a thing, where you can drink, smoke and curse and play pool, all the while surrounded by seemingly authentic movie memorabilia and bikers, assuming all the Harleys parked outside were real and not movie props. Oh and you can spit too! These days they have the only boat ramp on the bay side in that general area and they like to exploit that monopoly to the tune of twenty dollars for a daily park and launch ticket. I wasn't anticipating spending the night. After handing her a crisp new bill from the ATM, she wished me "tight lines" assuming that I was planning to fish. I decided not to challenge her assumption that I was a piscatologist, as I was certainly dressed and outfitted like one. I didn't want to creep her out and tell her that I was on an archeological reconnaissance mission, so I thanked her for her good wishes. I kept to myself my random thoughts that I thought my hat looked more like that of an archeologist. As the saying goes,

"So Many Books. So little time". In this instance, the saying should go "So few hats! So many gists!"

In the narrow Florida Keys which stretch for more than 100 road miles and require the crossing of over forty bridges, waterfront properties are designated as either "Bayside" or "Oceanside". Florida Bay which is a part of the Gulf of Mexico is on the right as you travel south to Key West and the Atlantic

Ocean and all of the famous diving reefs, shipwrecks and

lighthouses are on the left. Where you launch and what kind of

vessel you put in matters as it is not always possible to go from one

side to the other, except at strategic crossings which are few and

far between. Those accommodating sailboats with tall masts are

even fewer and further between. There is a narrow canal that

accommodates boats no more than 14 feet tall, called "Adam's

Cut" in Key Largo, which takes one into Largo Sound at John

Pennekamp National Park and provides access to the Atlantic and

the famous diving and snorkeling reefs, including the famous

"Christ of the Deep" statue via the park's excursion boat channel.

My destination this time around however was the Nest Keys

in the southeast quadrant of Everglades National Park. For Gertie

this would be a piece of cake at about a 20 mile round trip. While

I had no intention of kayaking all the way there and back, I did

want to paddle the surrounding water. The harness that was rigged

up to Gertie's stern cleats had my little eight foot blue Mainstream

Jazz kayak riding high and dry behind. At 13 feet, Gertie served as

the mother ship to the expedition. Upper Nest Key has one of the few island beaches in Everglades National Park and it is a designated overnight camping area (though one has to reserve a site and pay a fee). I like to think it is far enough away from the crocodiles over in Flamingo, or at least I like to tell myself that. As the self-styled "Man Who Seeks Beaches" guy I had to see this beach because it was there. There are very few beaches in the Florida Keys and when there is one, one is duty bound to at least check it out. The island is also home to some very unusual and incongruous architecture that rises ten feet above sea level that I had to see for myself.

My 2013 Google Earth routing had Gertie passing very close to a small, shallow body of water almost completely surrounded by land, which itself was surrounded by water. It looks like an atoll and is named Little Buttonwood Sound. It was this name that jogged my memory and over the decades that followed since the original Darryls' adventure, I had commingled the names with its neighbor, the similar sounding Blackwater Sound. The latter is also a book title made famous as the featured locale in a series of crime thrillers by Florida novelist, professor and poet, James W. Hall, whose recurring lead character is a fellow named Thorn.

Thorn has all the best attributes of Spencer, Travis McGee, Doc Ford, Dave Robicheaux and James Bond rolled into one and he doesn't suffer fools well at all. I shudder to think of what he might of thought of the Darryl's in his home body of water, though one hopes that the fact that the character wasn't "born" until 1987 would cut us some slack.

Back in 1988, toward sunset of the second day out, we entered the calm bay of Little Buttonwood Sound seeking an anchorage for the night. The first night had been spent in the lee of a couple of small no-name islands. A very large power yacht was leaving the Sound through the narrow cut at the same time as we were entering and the Captain shouted across that he had been unable to find a good holding ground for his anchor and thus he was not going to stay the night. Night was fast approaching and the brothers Darryl of course had no idea what he meant and confidently thought that was his problem for having such a big boat. When we threw the anchor off the bow, it disappeared in the ground underwater, which appeared to us as what anchors were meant to do, and everything was as it should be. It was approaching dusk and as a Canadian raised boy I wasn't able to resist the idea of swimming outdoors in

February. While wearing a mask and snorkel and swimming on the surface of the crystal clear water that was only two or three feet deep, a huge buried sting ray rose out of the marl directly under my torso. Its tail missed my chest by inches. Though a little freaked out, at the time I had no idea of the mortal danger I had been in, until about a decade ago when Steve Irwin, the Australian nicknamed the "Crocodile Hunter" was killed under very similar circumstances. We proceeded to debate all the big issues of the day, drink some whiskey and beer, play poker, smoke a lot and then retired to our respective bunks.

When I awoke I knew instinctively that something was wrong. The tree branches coming in through the windows were another indication. Apparently, even though we had never been to sea, we had been blown ashore. During our orientation for the houseboat rental, the manager (and much of the literature) made it clear that any ingestion of mud into the boat motor would result in fatal damage for which the renters (read Darryls) would be held liable. So one's first instinct which was to gun the engine out of the mangroves was off the table. I quietly slipped over the stern deck into the water with the hope that I could pull the shallow drafted vessel back out to deeper water before the others awoke. I could then pretend like nothing had happened. Unfortunately I promptly sank to my armpits in the marly muck. Luckily I had hold of a line or I might have been like one of those guys going down the quicksand pit in those old Tarzan movies. After pulling myself back up on to the deck of the boat and having a discussion with the crew as to our least expensive options we decided to all get in the water and pull the "Roger B" out of the mangroves. Though six of us hauling a line over our shoulders like Volga boatmen ought to have resulted in some advantage none of us could get a purchase in the mud and we were not able to move the boat even an inch. Back aboard, Schwartz ever philosophical opined on the nature of leadership and how any single person could lead five otherwise normally smart people into mud up to their armpits to risk their lives for a rented houseboat.

One of my favorite movies of all time is FITZCARRALDO by Werner Herzog in which the protagonist played by Klaus Kinski carries out an audacious scheme to manually haul a steamship across a mountain to link up to an Amazon tributary that flowed to a different watershed in the opposite direction. Subsequently over the next five or ten years our own little week-end excursion in Florida Bay took on epic proportions with each retelling and we dubbed it "Fitzbernardo" with me cast as either Klaus or Larry depending on how far you wanted to take the metaphors.

Chris radioed the boat charter office and apprised them of the predicament of the "Roger B". He also reassured them of our complete incredulity as to how this might have happened as well as our total lack of culpability in the matter. They promptly sent out a tow boat, the all cash fee for which would be our responsibility. The towing service was called "Blackbeard's Towing". This is one of the things I like about the Florida Keys. They are populated by rogues, iconoclasts, pirates, descendants of marine salvagers, "square grouper" fishermen or just plain folks who tried to get as far south from the rest of our country as they could, in order to do whatever it is they wanted to do that for whatever reason they couldn't do at home. They make no bones about the fact that the living they have to make is a zero sum game where they try to separate you from your money in as nice a way as possible, and failing that, in any way possible. Like their forebears, the marine salvers who eked a living out of others' ignorance, folly or misfortune, Florida Keys style highway robbery is merely a one

sided commercial exchange that is never in your favor and one

ought not to be offended. It is a food chain and those of us who

visit here are much further down. Whether it is the ridiculous cost

of tourist attractions, the sky-high cost of bed and board or the

phony wine based cocktails served on Duval St., you take it

because you want to be there and that is the price of admission.

Like the price of a beer at a ballpark or the daily admission ticket to Disney World, you know it is a rip-off, but you pay it with a smile. It is what you expected.

This towing service could have been called Sunshine Towing or Dependable Marine Services, or Acme Towing but no it was named after a pirate and we were about to get robbed. After having agreed to $125 on the radio, the pirate then charged us $150 ($300 in today's value), because he could. We took up a collection of tens and twenties and when he was done, he had moved our boat less than ten yards. Most importantly the brothers Darryl were free to pursue their adventure. We said good bye to Little Buttonwood Sound and headed out into Blackwater Sound (though at the time we knew the name of neither) looking for even more adventure and were forever more well acquainted with the term "holding ground" in the nautical sense.

"Anchors? Darryls don't need no stinkin' anchors!"

Somewhere in Florida Bay on our last night out in the "Roger B" we were all still awake well into the early morning hours. In the damp, cold, pre-dawn haze, a ghostly figure was spotted coming from behind a neighboring island and walking in the shallow water. Indeed it was an eerie sight worthy of a horror

movie as it looked as if the monster of the deep was walking on the

water and headed directly for us. Schwartz who often exhibited

paranoid symptoms under a wide variety of circumstances was

sure this fellow was going to kill us all and hijack our boat. I

reassured David that there were six of us and one of him and he

was not likely to be successful. We helped the man on board. A

typical "conch" or "cracker", apparently he had been out late

poaching in the Everglades and his boat engine had broken down.

He had been stranded since sundown the previous evening and had

seen our lights and started walking toward our boat. He had been

walking in the mud and water all night. Soaking wet, teeth

chattering and body shaking with the cold of the February night he

was undoubtedly suffering from hypothermia. After helping him

aboard, we wrapped a blanket around his shoulders and offered

him a hot cup of coffee which he could barely hold. At this point,

I'll admit that the movie plots of CAPE FEAR and KEY LARGO

flashed through my brain. He was very admiring of our boat and

mentioned how nice it was. Upon his second mention, I reviewed

those films again and thought perhaps Schwartz might have a

point. The man also asked what we did for a living, and when we told him we were booksellers, it seemed that he had little concept of such labor or how the fruits of it might result in a boat such as this one even if it was a rental. He wasn't satisfied until he concluded that of course we sold pornography. That seemed to settle it for him. We gave him some more time to recover and then one of us, asked him his name.

"Darryl" he replied.

Our howls of spontaneous laughter echoed throughout the bay for a very long and awkward time. Subsequently we had to explain to the poor real Darryl that we were not laughing at him. As he had never heard of Bob Newhart (likely spending too much time on poaching and porn) he couldn't get the joke and we remained embarrassed until we dropped him at a place along the highway on our way north out of the Florida Keys back to the cold winters to be found a few hours later in Chicago, Milwaukee, Toronto and New York.

The Nest Keys which I visited in 2013 are the islands of the Darryls' first night at anchor in 1988. I didn't want to leave you with the impression that there hadn't been any changes in thirty years between adventures in this same body of water. As it is all a part of the National Parks system, there is still no development on this part of Florida Bay. There is a proposal to ban gasoline outboard motors from this section of Everglades National Park, so "Darrylesque" trips by bumbling adventurers of future generations would become a thing of the past. There was some development that was heart-stopping and mind boggling both. There where everything around is flat, at the end of the dock were twin blue fiberglass structures soaring ten feet above sea level, the highest reference point for miles around. If these towering blue plastic landmarks had existed back then, we might have known where we were. We would certainly not have needed to wander aimlessly around Florida Bay using a hard edge Canadian cigarette pack for a parallel rule and for sure would never have met the real Darryl. We could have tied up right there for the duration and had all the necessary comforts.

GATOR BOY

During the better part of the decade I spent hanging around the Clam Pass parking lot or at the resort's swimming pool turning station, there were nearly always alligators in residence at the adjacent pond. At times there was just one, at other times as many as four or five. That pond is connected to other ponds in the neighborhood via underground pipes or canals or swales as part of the county government's elaborate rainwater detention system which is designed to let rain water run-off settle before releasing it to enter the salt water estuary. This is obviously a very good thing as most of the impurities, detritus and litter that wash off the city streets and parking lots are gathered in a finite space like a holding pond and settle out over time. It serves a double purpose too as the flow of freshwater which can be prodigious in the summer rainy season can be regulated by dams, weirs or gates before it is allowed to enter the estuary. An estuary is a food source for marine life and like a good soup broth it needs just the right amount of salt. Too much and the soup is ruined.

Too little and it is too bland to sustain marine life. The nature of

the water in the estuarine broth is called brackish and may be

stained brown, red or yellow as with tea. Some people mistakenly

conclude that it is dirty which may or may not be the case,

depending on how much leaf matter and detritus has settled out.

The color alone, as with tea or coffee is not necessarily an

indication of its cleanliness.

Generally alligators do not tolerate salt water well. That's why

they like to stay in freshwater and why people in Florida shouldn't

swim in lakes, rivers, creeks or bays. However, in the rainy season

when the freshwater is moving, the bays become less saline and

alligators are known to wander from one habitat to the other. One

year, the Clam Pass Estuary (almost all of which is in the Pelican

Bay neighborhood) was said to have had more than 60 alligators in

it. The Pelican Bay Berm road, the traffic on which is restricted to

golf carts, bicycles and pedestrians runs for more than two miles

on a north south axis. It was designed as a levy or dike and as one

is travelling north, the freshwater is kept to the right, or the town

side and the saltwater to the left, or the gulf side. Periodically, bridges and underpasses let the water flow in both directions and if an alligator is not impressed with a particular passage, it will just climb up the slope and walk over to the other side. Like the snakes, they too may interrupt their crossing of the path to bask on the heated surface. It's a fine line between harassment of an alligator and trying to shoo her off the path so the people can get to the beach. I can see why the alligator might get annoyed as she warms her cold blood on the hot pavement.

As with the snakes in the trees, when there was only one alligator, it was hard to tell if it was the same one or a different one and unlike big old tail-less "Stubby" just a mile north on the Berm road, these usually were younger with no such distinguishing marks having yet been acquired. It was also hard to tell if Reggie or Waldo had been removed or just swum away when they weren't there the next day.

For the more than two decades that the resort was named "The Registry" the resident alligator was called "Reggie" though in all likelihood it was "Reggie I", "Reggie II" or "Reggie III". Management usually let them grow to about 4 feet in length, after which they might call the "Gator Hot Line" to have them removed for liability reasons. During the Waldorf Astoria period I would call him "Waldo" as everyone always wanted to know where he was. When one calls the "nuisance gator hotline", it is invariably a death sentence for the alligator. It doesn't take much to be considered a nuisance if you are an alligator. Unfortunately, sometimes just being in the wrong place at the wrong time will do it, like under a park bench when a tourist is sitting on it, for example, or scoping out what the folks are unloading from their trunks in the adjacent parking lot. Florida Fish and Wildlife (FWC) authorizes euthanizing up to 7,000 alligators a year for being a nuisance so unless one honestly feels threatened it is better not to call. Our "Go To" alligator guy is known as Ray the Trapper and if you should ever find yourself in need of his services, he has a Facebook page.

Alligator trappers need to be licensed and are not paid for their services per se, but they benefit from selling the reptiles to farmers who will eventually harvest the meat and the hide. Once I watched as Ray stalked a fairly large five footer that had wandered into the parking lot and in the process innocently offended a group of tourists who were unloading beach gear from their cars. There was no question that this one had "bought the farm" and was headed there on the express. On another occasion though, when he was rounding up a congregation of small ones mostly about a foot long, he revealed to me that when they are this young and have had limited human contact, he takes it upon himself to drive them into the everglades and release them into the wild thus giving them a second chance at life. I thought this was an unusually enlightened attitude from a trapper, but perhaps not. The faces of conservation have changed a lot over a generation or two and after all the little alligators couldn't help it if they were hatched a half mile from a Saks Fifth Avenue and a Nordstrom, instead of a half mile from a Seminole Chickee Hut.

Invariably a conversation about alligators leads to one about crocodiles. Florida does indeed have crocodiles, not too many mind you, but enough to merit your attention. While the state has done an admirable job of aiding in the substantially successful recovery of the alligator population to more than one and a half million, they haven't had nearly as much success with the American Crocodile. It may have something to do with the fact that crocs love to hang out on the beaches and that just wouldn't be very good for business. As it is, there are now an estimated 2,000 in Florida with most residing in and around the Turkey Point nuclear power plant near Homestead on Florida's south east coast, where they live in a highly restricted area and appear to thrive as a direct result of the lack of human contact. Nameless wags, also suggest that radiation when mixed with nuclear waste and fertilizer run-off from the mega sugar plantations just north of them provide perfect conditions for growing crocodiles, similar to the sewers of New York as it relates to alligators.

If you've always wondered what a group of crocodiles is known as, it is called a "float" while a group of alligators is known as a "congregation". If you want to know what a group of anything and everything is called, I'd refer you to a book authored by an old professional acquaintance of mine from New York, James Lipton.

His book, "An Exaltation of Larks" has been continuously in print for more than 50 years.

There is a float of 11 crocodiles in the restricted area of Marco Island Airport (which is on the mainland) within hailing distance of the runway. A couple of these wander from time to time and there have been confirmed sightings as far inland as Davis Blvd in the King's Lake neighborhood. While gunkholing in one of my regular saltwater lagoons in back of Keewaydin Island, my daughter Lauren and I saw one there as well one Thanksgiving week-end a few years ago. Initially I mistook it for an alligator, but on a second and third look, the pointed snout, toothy overbite and highly pronounced fluked tail confirmed to me that it was a crocodile. As we were in Gertie with just 6 inches of freeboard above the waterline, we scrambled out of there in short order. It is very likely this was a wanderer from the Marco Island float which is only about 12 miles away from here as the tern flies. As far as is known, these are the only crocodiles in this neck of the woods though a tagged happy wanderer from Homestead was found in Naples in 2008 and returned there only to be found later near Tampa. They do not do well in a frost so they are generally found south of Fort Myers. There was a 50 something year old female

for years at Ding Darling Sanctuary in Sanibel, but she died in the

freeze of 2009. There are more in the Flamingo area of Everglades

National Park in and around Florida Bay and along the beach at

Cape Sable and in the estuaries behind it. There are also

substantial populations in the Dominican Republic and Cuba, as

well as the Western Caribbean, coastal Mexico, Central America

and northern Latin America.

Two young boys, one perhaps 14 years of age and the

other 16 or 17, were fishing in the parking lot pond near the hotel

turning station. People usually fish out at Clam Pass for game fish

such as Snook, Redfish, Spanish Mackerel, Black Drum, Sea Trout

or Sheepshead among other species. In my experience they didn't

usually fish in this puny pond where there may be some bream,

sunfish or small bass and a big old snapping turtle. Besides there

were thousands of ponds just like this one all over the county and

if they were Florida boys, there was likely one in their own

backyard. However, they did appear to have just returned from the

beach as the younger boy had a beach blanket and I thought

perhaps they were just killing some time waiting for their ride home. After a couple of round trips, my curiosity got the better of me.

"Hi fellas. Any luck?"

"No Sir. Not yet!"

"You're casting awfully close to that gator. Be careful now. You don't want to hook him by accident. That would be a heck of a mess."

"Yes Sir. No Sir."

And so off I went to the beach again and on my return trip, as I crossed the short bridge from the boardwalk to the hotel turning circle, I passed the two boys walking towards the parking lot. They were walking quite briskly and the younger one was wearing his beach blanket draped over his left shoulder, serape style. This struck me as odd and it was. Just under the hemline of the blanket, what appeared to be a tail dangled out at knee height. I u-turned at the station, discharged my passengers and followed the boys to their car in the public parking lot.

"What do you have under that blanket?"

"Nuthen."

"You've got something under that blanket. Let me see what it is or I'll call the Ranger right now."

Reluctantly, he acquiesced and there perched like a parrot on the shoulder that had been under the blanket was a three foot long juvenile alligator with jaws duct taped shut.

"Man what were you thinking?"

"I dunno."

So far the older boy who was apparently the driver of the car and had opened the trunk to put the alligator inside had been completely quiet so I addressed him instead.

"Are you guys brothers?"

"Cuzzins."

"You know he's kind of young, but you are old enough to know better. Are you from around here?"

"Yeah. We live out in the Estates."

"What were you going to do with him?"

"We've got a canal in the back of the house and we've always wanted to have our own gator."

"Well, you know you can't keep wild animals as pets and as Florida boys you for sure know that you aren't allowed to harass or handle alligators. You know this is a serious offense."

"Yessir."

"If I call FWC, and I should, you are going to be in a heap of trouble."

"Yessir."

"You seem like nice guys, but you've got a few loose screws. I'll tell you what. You put that alligator back over there in that pond where you got him right now and we'll just forget this ever happened."

At the time, I thought this was the right thing to do for the alligator and the boys. Later, as I learned more, I have become convinced that it was not. Not because the boys weren't taught a hard lesson like some would argue they should have been, but because by returning this gator to this pond, he was doomed. He couldn't really live a full life in public view in a public park and even if he hadn't been handled by humans, sooner rather than later, (he was already three feet long) he would be deemed a nuisance and euthanized. Frankly he stood a much better chance at having a longer life in a canal in Golden Gate Estates, though it is just as likely he might have spent his entire life there harried and harassed as a quasi-family pet being fed table scraps. It's an age old conundrum isn't it? Better to be free and perhaps dead in short order, or be kept and live to a ripe old age on metaphorical table scraps.

Bernard Rath

BATS IN THE BELFRY

You may wish to take issue with my use of the word belfry here as there are no bells, though there could be and as long as there is a space for a bell, even a small one, then technically it is one. There were definitely bats in it and I am not one to pass up an opportunity for an alliterative title with so many cinematic, musical and literary references.

I started working here in the spring of 2005, when the gazebo's roof was still intact. It was made of cedar shakes, which is likely not the best choice for roofing material in the hot, humid and wet Florida climate. In addition to the moss growing on it, over the period of the next seven or eight years the shakes began to rot. At the apex of the roof was a copper cone with a small opening for ventilation at the bottom of it. A thriving colony of Brazilian free-tailed bats had established residency up inside the cone and prospered. According to the longest tenured tram driver there when I joined the crew, the bats had resided in the gazebo for most of the two decades since it had been built. During the dusk period in the evenings after the sun had set, the colony would be out in mass flying very close to the roof of my tram, while managing to stay beneath the mangrove canopy. In my estimation flying in the dark was no mean feat. By using echolocation, their ability to perceive their environment surpasses that of most humans. I don't know if it was as good for them as it was for me, but it was terrific for me while it lasted. It was the strangest sensation, like being on the set of a National Geographic nature documentary. It is well known that a single insect eating bat can consume up to 500 mosquitoes in an hour of feasting. In all those months and years of working the sunset shift in a saltwater marsh, I never had a single mosquito bite, an amazing fact that I attribute to this wonderful colony or to the Pelican Bay Services Division mosquito control spraying program. I prefer to credit the bats. On the other hand, they didn't seem to have nearly the same effect on the biting midge (no-see-um) population and those of us out there around sunset each night regularly received more than our fair share of their dastardly attention. No-see-ums are so slight that if even a modest breeze is blowing then they can't land on you and do their thing and if we couldn't "see um" then it is not surprising that the bats couldn't either. Honestly though, I expected more given that they have the added benefit of echolocation. I guess the tiny, flimsy midges don't throw off much of an echo and besides with a banquet of mosquitoes presenting itself each night, why bother with the crumbs. Most people don't realize that biting midges don't all bite as such. Nor do they necessarily sting. There are more than 4,600 different kinds of biting midges and many kinds have their own unique way to annoy us. Often they don't bite but may secrete an acidic substance on your skin that burns you and feels like a sting or a bite. When in the evenings people complained about being bitten I was able to reassure them that such was not the case and if they looked closely they would not see a break in their skin. Ever helpful, I would point out that they had likely been "peed" upon by an insect. It was a small comfort, but the best I could do under the circumstances. Nature can be cruel.

A Funny Thing Happened On The Way To The Beach

The busiest time of the day for beach goers is when the sun is high in the sky. Unfortunately, this is when the bats were in residence and trying to catch some shut-eye after a long night spent hunting mosquitoes on our behalf in the mangroves. The noises, the chirping and the droppings coming from the ventilation hole began to attract attention as the colony grew in size and people began to take notice. Then every now and again, a pup would lose its grip and fall to the pavement and generally not survive the ordeal, though on a few occasions, it did. It was important that people not handle the bats and we would use an empty cardboard box and turn it upside down to cover the bat as we waited for help to arrive in the form of volunteers often led by Tom Cravens, a nearby resident, bat expert and volunteer from the Conservancy of Southwest Florida. He would handle them gingerly and bring them to the wildlife rescue center and try to nurse them back to health though at times, it was necessary to euthanize them. Over time, the cedar shake roof began to deteriorate from the outside. As holes began to appear, the chirping in the colony attracted big crows, some almost the size of ravens that used their big beaks and talons to carve out even bigger openings to get at the seemingly endless supply of delectable mousey snacks inside. They had a great deal of success and we tram drivers often looked on helplessly as one or another of the crows flew away with a squealing bat. While it was nature at work, it was more than I cared to see and on occasion I would find a stone and throw it at a crow on the roof. Unfortunately, like all mammals, bats are vectors for the deadly rabies virus but the likelihood of them actually passing along the virus is vastly overstated. However now that they were no longer "out of sight, out of mind" in the dark of the woods, people began to be concerned for their own safety and that of their children. And so was born a vicious and mostly successful campaign to eradicate the bats from the belfry in the Clam Pass Gazebo, by of all people, the local park ranger.

Growing up, perhaps I had an overly idealistic vision of what a park ranger was, brought on in all likelihood by Smokey the Bear. My Canadian Boy Scout hat looked exactly like his and there was a time when I seriously considered going to Forestry School and standing in a tower to scan the horizon for smoke somewhere in the millions of square miles of Canadian forests. At least two of my high school classmates became Mounties and got the hat, while I became a book salesman and also got a hat. Mine was and still is, a beautiful, authentic Ecuadorean made Panama hat, acquired while visiting New Orleans for the first time in October of 1979.

In my opinion, park rangers ought to be conservation minded and friends of Bambi and Thumper and all the creatures of the forest. People often asked me what kind of wildlife there was in the mangrove forest and I would answer glibly and truthfully that there were snakes, bats and rats, a few raccoons and lots of spiders. I know they were disappointed because they wanted me to say that Bambi and Thumper lived there in harmonious bliss with all the other creatures of the forest, but that wasn't the case. Park rangers need to be friends of all the creatures, not just the cuddly ones and their responsibility is no less real in a mangrove forest than it is in a forest comprised of oaks, maples, beeches or redwoods. So, imagine my shock when I discovered that my local park ranger had taken it upon herself to personally eradicate all the bats in the belfry because they were potential rabies carriers. Technically, so is everything mammalian that moves. Of course, so are the many raccoons that pop in and out of the waste baskets on the boardwalk all night long, yet to my knowledge no-one tried to eradicate them.

From time to time, someone might attempt a relocation program.

One year they humanely trapped and relocated about a half dozen

of them and in 2015 Pelican Bay authorities relocated seven of

them from the area around Marker 36. Had they chosen that

option with the bats, I wouldn't have objected in the least.

Yellow crime scene tape, strung around the perimeter of the

gazebo, greeted me as I arrived at work one morning. An inverted

orange traffic cone was stuffed into the opening of the apex to keep

the bats from getting either in or out. If the cone had been installed

during daylight hours, the bats would have been trapped inside, though the holes in the roof would have likely kept them from

suffocating quickly. On the other hand, if the cone had been

installed at night, then our colony would have become homeless

after their next foraging foray and pups left inside would have

slowly died of starvation. There was a strong chemical smell about

and I was afraid that they had also been gassed, though I had no

proof of that. Nevertheless, I was livid and fit to be tied and called

the Conservancy and someone called someone else and within a

few hours, the cone had been removed, but the damage to the

colony might have been permanent. Not too long after that, the

Parks department re-roofed the gazebo station and the colony

disappeared. Subsequently the parks department in conjunction

with the Conservancy and guidance from Tom Cravens installed a

proper bat house on the top of a slippery metal pole intended to foil

those same pesky raccoons. It is located in the middle of an

adjacent freshwater marsh, the water source for which is the

overflow from the nearby alligator pond. It is there for all to see,

but at the time of publication, remained unoccupied. Not too long

after re-roofing the gazebo, the parks department decided to raze

the old structure and build a new one anyway. It sports a beautiful tin roof that gets very hot in the Florida sunshine and there are

neither bats under it nor cats on it. Heaven knows what the

authorities will do if the latter should ever occur.

UNDER THE BOARDWALK

"Wait! He can't do that can he?"

"Do what?"

"That!"

I was just about to pull out of the beachside round-about, when the woman shouted. Peering into the mirror, the woman in the second row was clearly visible, but I couldn't discern the object of her concern.

"The boy on the back of the tram is stealing a turtle."

The bench at the rear of the tram faces in the opposite direction. I walked to the back of the vehicle and sure enough, there sat a boy of college age with a great big grin on his face and a great big gopher tortoise on his lap. It seemed that he wanted a pet for his dorm and this free, wizened, low maintenance beauty fit the bill perfectly. Many species of tortoises are kept as pets and you can buy them on-line from breeders and stores. One of those, this size might cost many hundreds of dollars. Not this one though as Gopher Tortoises' conservation status is "Threatened and Vulnerable".

"Son. The lady is right. You can't do that."

"But I'll take good care of him."

"Well that's kind of neither here nor there, because you just can't do that. In fact, you are not even supposed to handle them."

"Now just go put him back exactly where you found him and we'll get on our way."

This wasn't the first time that an intervention to save the life of a Gopher Tortoise from an unsuspecting and/or well meaning visitor to Florida, was called for. On numerous occasions I've had to step in to save a tortoise from being thrown into the ocean to drown. Tortoises live on land and have claws on their legs for digging and not flippers for swimming. They use their claws to dig elaborate burrows, some between 40 and 50 feet long. The area behind the beach at Clam Pass Park is riddled with active and abandoned burrows. Hundreds of other species are dependent upon the abandoned burrows, when seeking their own shelter and habitat.

"Excuse me girls, where are you going with that?"

"We're bringing her back to the ocean. She looks all dried out. She's been out of the water way too long. She probably couldn't find her way back to the sea after she laid her eggs."

"Just put her back right there where you picked her up from. She lives here behind the restaurant under all those sand piles you see. She's a tortoise not a turtle."

"Oh my God. Sorrreeee!"

"Make sure you wash your hands really well."

The latter was a zinger I used to like to throw into the mix on occasion, to make sure that they didn't make a habit of picking up the wildlife for more fun in the sun. Actually, they should have washed their hands before handling the tortoise as the tortoise was more at risk from them than vice versa.

The tortoises are a big hit with kids and adults alike at Clam Pass. Over a period of years, some of them have grown and migrated from one set of burrows on the north of the round-about by the beach to the south side of it, a distance of perhaps twenty or thirty yards. On a slow day, when sitting and waiting for passengers I would often hear rustling coming from under the boardwalk as a gopher tortoise foraged for greenery under the piles of dried sea-grape leaves.

Generally speaking, I think people are disappointed in Gopher Tortoises. They really want them to be Sea Turtles.

The latter are very glamorous sophisticated world travelers whose little flippered babies make the nightly news and cause us all to dowse our lights at nine o' clock in the evening for most of the year. It's not the fault of the Gopher Tortoise that it is like many of us ungainly, drab, gray and wrinkled instead of shiny and sleek. I have seen baby Gopher Tortoises and they are really cute with a mottled yellow and brown shell so one can see first-hand what decades of lying in the hot sand and sun does to one's outer epidermal layers.

Still, unlike tortoises that never move more than a few yards from where they were born, sea turtles like Leatherbacks, Loggerheads, Ridleys, Greens and Hawksbills stir one's imagination. They deposit thousands of eggs each summer deep in the sand on Florida's many beaches and then head back to sea continuing their migrations. Leaving the eggs in the sand to their fate, the mom's head off to Europe for another season destined for exotic isles such as Madeira or Gran Canaria or the Azores for the winter, languidly floating on flotsam caught in the current of the Gulf Stream, all the while on the look-out for a hot date. At some point a couple of months later, against all odds the thousands of little ones make the middle of the night scamper for the moonlit gulf with no Mom or Dad to ever show them the way.

"How was your visit?. Did you enjoy the beach?" said I to a nice lady likely from Chicago, Minneapolis, Indianapolis, Columbus or Cleveland or Toronto or some such place.

"Oh yes. It was the best day. A sea turtle was lying on her nest right next to me, hatching her babies".

I just let it go. After all there is only so much explaining one can do and still be expected to drive a tram safely. Besides why ruin her "best day".

MONKEY IN THE MANGROVES

The tram ride through the woods is similar in a lot of ways to some of the amusement park rides in different parts of Florida. People have compared it to the Jurassic Park theme ride at Universal Studios in Orlando or Disney's Jungle Cruise. It has also been compared to Jungle Larry's. During the 1960's, Jungle Larry and his wife Safari Jane, (likely not their real names) merged their collection of exotic animals into an existing collection of exotic botanicals, which after a few different iterations ultimately metamorphosed into the Naples Zoo we all know and love today. Our zoo has a very popular monkey boat ride and one of our former Clam Pass tram drivers these days commands one of the "Monkey Boats" as we like to call them. Technically, it is a primate boat ride as the islands are also home to lemurs and apes.

The science of last century posited for the longest time that monkeys couldn't swim, thus the half dozen or so little Alcatraz's that are only reachable by boat in the Caribbean Garden ponds. The science of the 21st century however has concluded that many monkeys and apes do swim and may have been doing so for quite some time. This could explain a number of things, not the least of which is the well substantiated story that a troop of feral monkeys that may have been descended from escapees from the zoo did exist, somewhere between the Gordon River and the Collier Athletic Club on Goodlette-Frank Road in the city of Naples. At least one Duffy Electric Boat guide who volunteers for the Conservancy of SW Florida reports having seen them during the past decade or so, but not lately. It might also help explain away my nightmares of surreptitiously swimming simians storming my kayak while I am being chased down a narrow mangrove tunnel in the Gordon River behind the zoo by an eight foot alligator that had decided I had gone far enough. The simians were like those nasty winged ones in the Wizard of Oz movie.

A mangrove estuary is not a very hospitable environment for most mammals as there is little freshwater to drink and there are no fruit bearing trees as such. Between the exotic Brazilian Pepper

plants and the native Black Mangroves, the leaves of which glisten

with salt, condiments though are in generous supply. So, if you

like salt and pepper, you'd be all set in a mangrove forest, though

you would likely have to dig for the clams and bring in the butter.

The Clam Pass estuary could support mammalian life though as

"The Berm" which runs the entire length of the estuary from south

to north in Pelican Bay, acts as a dike in retaining freshwater to the

east of it. So mammals and monkeys could drink and survive. So

I suppose that could explain why there was a monkey in the

mangroves when I went to work one day.

He, she or it was up in the trees and swinging around from

here to there with, as Chuck Berry once said " no particular place

to go". I have been advised not to use the real names of people in

my writing in that they might take umbrage at their portrayal. This

of course does not apply to the brothers Darryl who take pride in

any mention of their antics and wouldn't know the meaning of the

word in any case. Fortunately, one of our former tram drivers is a

veteran of the Vietnam War's encryption service who was helpful

in devising a code to keep the drivers' privacy and anonymity intact. As his service to this day, almost 50 years later is still classified, I have to refer to him as Retep, though it pains me not to be able to give him proper credit.

I have since forgotten which driver it was, but I vaguely recollect that it was Nor, who is the brother of the Monkey Boat Captain Nod, who made the initial discovery. We were all enthralled and excited and became even more so when the monkey came down from the trees, perched on the rail next to us, tilted its cute little head and with its big eyes seemed to ask for something. Naturally, we thought it might want something to eat so we drove out to the restaurant which was then called Paradise Grill at Clam Pass and scavenged whatever was on hand, mostly lemon, lime and orange slices hitherto destined for touristy tropical drinks without in this case straws or umbrellas. It pleased us all that the monkey ate everything we brought its way. None of us took it upon ourselves to determine the monkey's gender and this was well before Bruce and Caitlin and the current insouciance with regard to gender issues. In the interests of minimizing awkwardness in pronouns in this re-telling let's just call he/she/it, an IT, sort of like

ET. Frankly none of us knew the gender of Steven Spielberg's ET, and as I recall it wasn't critical to the story.

Having punted on the gender question, it now fell upon the assembled tram drivers to determine the species of monkey represented by "Big Eyes". All of us considered ourselves experts in every aspect of mangrove jungle lore and as a result each of us concluded that it was a different species of monkey. My best guess was that it was a capuchin, which is the kind of monkey associated with organ grinders, and to this day years later I am sticking to it. Others decided that it was a spider monkey, which looked nothing like it all in my opinion. Both species were known to have been deployed as service animals and since this monkey was but a hundred yards or so from the Glenview, an upscale "continuing care" high rise in Pelican Bay, I thought it reasonable to surmise that IT was likely an escapee from there.

That was no mean feat, as I would often refer to the Glenview as the Hotel California, as in the Eagles song where you could check out but you could never leave. To my knowledge no human had ever escaped from there and IT might have been the only mammal ever to have successfully done so. Periodically I would go into what I perhaps mistakenly thought was an entertaining riff

as to whether one checked in at the first floor and worked one's

way to the penthouse and then had one's ashes scattered

ceremoniously or otherwise from the penthouse balcony, or if one

entered by way of the penthouse and then worked one's way down

and was unceremoniously removed out the back door, when the

"continuing care" was inevitably "discontinued".

Generally speaking one isn't likely to get into the Glenview on

a tram driver's pay grade so the use of the higher balconies to

scatter one's ashes over the mangroves is likely out of reach to the

average park visitor or employee. One tram driver of very long

standing managed to convince his family, (against their better

judgment I'd expect) to launch his ashes from the Rube Goldberg

inspired draw bridge. Luckily there was a "C" breeze blowing that

day. The authorities generally frown upon that sort of thing and

want people to go further off-shore, but that doesn't work so well

for many people, most of whom don't have access to a boat. Some

people launch those Mylar or metallic, helium commemorative

balloons, but that is really irresponsible and environmentally destructive. I have picked up a dozen or more of them from the area beaches during my walks.

"Congratulations. Here flies Bernie. May he forever float above the beaches of Naples".

I get giddy, when I think of what an enterprising company like Amazon can do with this concept by employing drones. The possibilities are endless and likely lucrative. Most importantly, upon drone delivery of an appropriate, custom turned unique urn, one could fill it up with the remains on hand and send it back or have it jettisoned on the way to the repository over your old neighborhood. A "birds-eye" video documentary would be made available for an additional fee of course.

It is likely, that this ash scattering practice is happening a lot more than we think and people just aren't talking about it for obvious reasons. I mean if everyone started doing this along the shallow coastal waters we would likely run the risk of a new environmental threat. "Global Coagulation", is the term I have coined, for the net effect of this irresponsible practice which if we don't act now will inevitably lead to an altered coastal eco-system.

Shallow estuaries would become thick with coagulants, threatening the fragile food chain. There are three and a half million people in Florida over 65 according to recent census figures and a lot of them are of the notorious self-centered Baby Boom generation that brought society soaring deficits, depleted social security accounts and legal marijuana. They aren't likely to spring for the one way ticket back up north, especially now that there is often a fee imposed for carry-on baggage. If just half of them chose "scattering" then that is a lot of coagulants with which future generations will have to grapple.

My recollection is that the monkey stayed with us for a good amount of time. Nor recollects that it was there for less than week. Whatever it was, it was a wonderful time. The kids on the tram absolutely loved it, their parents were incredulous and whenever we mentioned it, people thought we were putting them on. We would chirp and offer fruits (we brought bananas from the employee cafeteria to supplement the citrus from the beach grill) and IT would show up. It was so good for business that I earnestly suggested that we get more of them. We could do a "Jungle Bernie's" and have monkeys everywhere and people would come from hundreds or even thousands of miles away to drive through

our mangrove forest. And then things went downhill again.

The secret was out and word was getting around town that there

was a monkey in the mangroves. It seems that monkeys are

mammals too and as vectors of rabies can be a serious health

hazard and so the real world intruded and required that IT be

removed, forthwith. The person that was going to be doing the

removing was once again the very same "Bat Lady Ranger". She

had saved the park patrons from the bats and had now taken it

upon herself to save them from the monkey. But she couldn't find

IT and didn't know where to look. Like Spanky and the Gang,

faced with the aloofness of the adult world, in a rare moment of solidarity the tram drivers united to protect our little friend from a certain bleak fate.

" I hear there is a monkey in the park. Take me to him" ordered the Ranger.

"Are you serious? That s crazy. There's no way. Who told you that?" responded the irreverent tram driver who'd obviously had trouble with authority from a very young age.

"Lots of people. Now take me to him. Monkeys spread disease and we need to capture it and remove it before it bites somebody."

"Look if there was a monkey in the park, we might not have seen it. This is a huge park. If he was here, he's probably moved on up the berm to Pelican Bay by now. They've got a much bigger menu up there in the Sandbar restaurant than we do in the Paradise Grill. If it was here, it likely found a better place to hang out."

"Are you saying that you have not seen a monkey?"

"You know my eyesight isn't what it used to be. I saw something, but it looked like a raccoon."

"Are you telling me that you can't tell the difference between a raccoon and a monkey?" said the Bat Lady Ranger.

"I'm in my sixties and don't wear my correct glasses as often as I should. They're both round, brown and furry right? That's all you're going to get from me."

Bat Lady Ranger turned her attention to Nor, the tram driver of panther fame from Chapter One who just happened to be passing by in the other direction. I suspected that just like with the panther, Nor had been neglecting his driving responsibilities to secretly play with the monkey and was likely working out a complicated plot to kidnap IT and bring it home to use as a "chick-magnet". Perhaps IT was already in his trunk.

"I haven't been working days much, but Nor has been. Hey Nor, did you see a monkey?" I called out in an effort to get myself off the Bat Lady Ranger's hook.

"Come on man, you know I quit drinking last month. Stop picking on me. What color was it?"

"Sort of beige, brownish blonde."

"Naw. I thought I might have seen one the other morning, but it was more pink. That's when I knew I had to quit drinking. You mean there really might be a monkey in here. I wasn't hallucinating after all? I gave up drinking vodka for no reason? Hey did you know vodka has no carbs?"

"You know, there are quite a few raccoons in here. From a distance, people could easily mistake a raccoon in a tree for a monkey in a mangrove tree."

"Well if you see it, call me right away!"

"Yes Ma'am. How come you don't capture all the raccoons in the park and remove them? They can be rabid too and they scare the heck out of everybody when they pop out of the garbage cans after dark."

"Don't know. I'm here for the monkey."

It is not the first time that in the interest of social justice a small lie was told to mislead authorities, the net effect of which is to obstruct their misguided or ill-intentioned state business. Generally speaking, Florida is not nice to monkeys. State lawmakers provide agricultural tax incentives and thus an hospitable environment for "Monkey Farms" though I fail to see what milking a cow and torturing a monkey have in common. These are often breeding operations to provide cannon fodder for research laboratories. One such farm in Hendry County, just east of Collier County was exposed by PETA in the summer of 2015. There were over 3,000 monkeys present. One of them, looked kind of like IT. It is said the Mounties (the Royal Canadian Mounted Police) always get their man. I am not sure if the Collier County Park Rangers always get their monkey but IT disappeared soon thereafter and the rest of the story remains a mystery. I will say this though. Give me a hundred monkeys like IT and a half dozen tram drivers like Nor and Nod and the Clam Pass Estuary would be the most popular tourist destination in and around Naples Florida.

AFTERWORD

I reluctantly stopped driving trams at Clam Pass Park at the end of November in 2014. After my virgin crossing of the Gulf Stream in a sailboat earlier that month, it seemed that I had put that off for way too long. At my age working full-time didn't allow me to do the many things that I still wanted to do within the allotted time. Writing, going on adventures and sailing are just some of those things. I now work seasonally as one of those red shirted security officers at Pelican Bay. I miss all of the regulars at Clam Pass Park and if one day you should find yourself looking north across the inlet and see a guy in a red shirt and white beard that looks like Santa Claus waving furiously, it's more likely me than him. Thanks for reading my tales.

"Good stories deserve a little embellishment"

JRR Tolkien

ABOUT THE ILLUSTRATOR

Margit Heiss is a talented Naples artist whose works are generally more abstract. The piece opposite is more representative of her style when she is on exhibit at the Gallery on Fifth in the Mercato Center in Naples Florida. Born and raised in southern Germany, where her closest beach was the muddy bank of Lake Chiemsee, she has lived in South Africa and Brazil. Those influences can be seen clearly in her work. We have been fortunate to have had her in Naples Florida since 2001. However, like the author, she is addicted to beaches of all sorts and has been kicking around the idea of living on an island. Whereas the author's is somewhere warm, hers is in the middle of a very old nasty sea that was featured in a well known 16th century play about a hurricane. She has a collection of the finest sands from the finest beaches around the world. The author sincerely thanks her for getting out of her comfort zone to enhance the readers' experience with this book.

Photo Credit: Lauren Rath

ABOUT THE AUTHOR

Bernard "Bernie" Rath is the only person to have served as Executive Director of two of the three North American booksellers associations. He was an early Internet retail pioneer and his reluctant decision to sell bookcases rather than books has turned out to be a success. He still sells them out of a 4th generation family owned factory in the foothills of the Adirondacks. He is an avid sailor and recently made his virgin Gulf Stream crossing at the age of 65 in a 41 foot catamaran. His amusing outdoor adventures from Florida's southwest coast to the Keys, the Bahamas and beyond can be found by doing a Google search for Florida Gunkholer. This is his second non-fiction book published and distributed by Amazon through its Kindle and Createspace companies.

REACH YOUR PERFECT BEACH IN
AND AROUND NAPLES FLORIDA

Everything you didn't know you wanted to know about
Collier County Florida's 35 miles of beaches

New Second Edition. Ilustrated with over 50 photographs and maps

Bernard Rath

AMAZON REVIEWS OF THE AUTHOR'S FIRST BOOK

"Rarely does one find a book so useful and yet so entertaining as Reach your Perfect Beach. I am a long-time kayaker (a veteran of the Wilderness Waterway) and Naples resident. This book not only led me to beach access points unfamiliar to me, it provided many amusing bits of Naples history in an engaging and wry style."

"A must read for both residents and visitors. Guaranteed to inform you about the area and answer questions that you wish were addressed in the typical tourist guides"

"Even if you think you are familiar with the beautiful beaches abounding in our little slice of paradise, Bernard provides the reader with concise instructions on the exploration of our abundant beaches. He includes many unknown facts and bits of wit and wisdom which the reader (even those unfamiliar with the area) should find enjoyable. I am eager to begin a much more thorough exploration of our gorgeous beaches with Bernard' s assistance!"

"Mr. Rath is an excellent story writer/story teller. I can't wait to walk Barefoot Beach"

"Bernard has given those of us from the North and Northwest a wonderful guide for exploration of the silicone wonders of Southwest Florida in Collier County. I found the book to be most helpful for someone who knew Sanibel and Captiva, but not our neighboring southern playground. I have come for many years to Southwest Florida and yet I found the guidance wonderfully entertaining and most helpful"

"Reach Your Perfect Beach is a thoroughly informative and entertaining travel guide to the best places to dip your toes in the sand and water of Collier County. A must read for both residents and visitors. Guaranteed to inform you about the area and answer questions that you wish were addressed in the typical tourist guides"

"Very informative book on the beautiful beaches of Naples FL"

PHOTO CREDIT OUTSIDE BACK COVER: Ray Morin

Made in the USA
Columbia, SC
09 March 2019